Lean Training Games in the OR

Gerard Leone
Richard D. Rahn

Flow Publishing, Inc.
Boulder, Colorado

Lean Training Games in the OR

By Gerard Leone, Richard Rahn

Published by:

Flow Publishing Inc.
7690 Watonga Way
Boulder, Colorado 80303
(303) 494-4693
www.flowpublishing.com
contact@flowpublishing.com

ISBN- 978-0-9833839-2-5

Table of Contents

Introduction

Just about everyone learns best by *doing.* A pilot, for example, needs to complete some classroom work, but much of the training will take place in the air and at the controls of a plane. This is good, but also time and fuel consuming, and a potentially risky use of an expensive resource, the plane. For that reason and more, commercial pilots log time in a *flight simulator.* While the simulator is not identical to actual flight, it is a valuable and much cheaper substitute for flight time. Dangerous procedures can be practiced over and over in a simulator, without putting the pilot and the hardware at risk, until the pilot response becomes "muscle memory".

In the same way, Lean training often includes hands-on exercises to demonstrate important Lean methods. In this case the term *simulation* refers to a classroom exercise that mimics the functioning of a real-world system, but in much less time and much less effort. Some common Lean simulations include the *Batch Versus Flow* exercise, where students will build a classroom "product" in batch mode and then in flow mode, and compare the results. These exercises can be real eye-openers for the students, because the performance difference between the two scenarios is so great. In the case of the Batch Versus Flow simulation, the same number of units can be built (with the same number of people) in flow mode in

1/10th of the time needed to build them in batch mode. This simulation is included in this book in Chapter 2.

Another eye-opening simulation included in this book is the *Par Versus Kanban* simulation in Chapter 1. If your hospital is using the Par Level method, and most are, you will be shocked at the difference between it and the Kanban method. Spoiler alert: Kanban wins!

Don't miss the opportunity to actually complete some real improvements, by taking your simulation directly to the "gemba", where the work is done. Ideally these simulations would be part of a Kaizen event, where the participants would be able to apply what they have learned immediately on a real-world opportunity. After all, if these methods are not going to be put into practice, then the training itself is a waste.

There are no limits to the possibilities for new simulations, and please share your ideas if you come up with a new one!

Gerard Leone
Richard D. Rahn

P.S. Here are some additional tools to try out online. Go to at www.leanhospitalgroup.com and select the "Tools" menu option. There are several games to try out there, including a Kanban Benefits simulator.

6 Lean Training Games in the OR

Chapter 1:
Par Level vs Kanban Simulation

Most hospitals today use the Par Level method to manage supplies. This system is fundamentally broken, but the force of habit is strong and the following simulation will shine a spotlight on the difference between it and the method of choice, Kanban. If you have Kanban skeptics in your group, fewer will remain after seeing this simple exercise. Just follow the instructions below. Note that this is a simplified version of a more in-depth simulation exercise in the *Par Versus Kanban Simulation Toolkit*, and the Kanban method itself is discussed in detail in our companion book *Supplies Management in the OR*. Both of these tools are available for sale at www.flowpublishing.com.

First gather the supplies you'll need:

1. One plastic bin.
2. Twenty poker chips, to represent supplies.
3. Two plastic zip-lock bags. We'll use them in the Kanban portion of the simulation.
4. The data collection worksheet. A link to this file is provided in Appendix 2 in the back of this book.
5. A stop watch.

6. A space to conduct the simulation, with enough room to walk around. A conference room or training room will be fine.

You will also need two physical locations within your training space, a Point of Use and a Central Stores. These areas should not be next to each other. Locate them on opposite sides of the room, in order to simulate the distance between the storeroom and the place where the supplies are used. Require some walking.

Prepare the data collection sheet (provided as a PDF):

METRIC	PAR	KANBAN	DIFF	%
Number of Supplies Counted Per Day				
Time Spent Counting Supplies (Seconds)				
Number of Replenishment Cycles (Trips)				
Time Spent Replenishing Supplies (Seconds)				
Distance Traveled (Feet or Meters)				
Total Elapsed Time				

As you can see, we'll be measuring the number of replenishment trips to and from central stores, the time required to replenish supplies, the number of counts and the time required to count, the distance walked and the total time.

This simulation will be conducted in two cycles, one as a Par Level simulation and the other in Kanban mode. You will need to staff the simulation with the following roles:

1. **A user**. This person will be consuming the supplies based on the schedule provided below. He/she will simply remove the required number of items from the bin or container. It is important to run both simulations under the same consumption pattern, in order to compare apples to apples.

2. **A data recorder.** This person will be managing the data collection sheet, and recording the results as they happen. You will be simulating five days of consumption, so the data recorder will keep a tally of the results for each day.

3. **A timer.** This person will be responsible for keeping track of the time (in seconds) for the various activities during the simulation, and to report results to the data recorder.

4. **A supplies handler**. This person will be restocking the supplies, using the Par Level method first and then the Kanban method. We'll explain the work in more detail below.

5. **A Master of Ceremonies**. This is usually the instructor, who will direct the activities of the simulation and give instructions to the participants as needed.

Place 10 poker chips or coins in the bin, in the Point of Use area. This is the actual Par Level for this bin. The Point of Use could represent an OR suite, a nursing floor, or anywhere that supplies are used in the hospital. Place the other 10 poker chips in the Central Stores area. This represents the supplier of the items, from which you will restock the Point of Use.

Running the Par Level Simulation

You will be simulating 5 days of consumption, based on the following usage:

Day	Quantity Used
Monday	2
Tuesday	2
Wednesday	4
Thursday	2
Friday	1

The Master of Ceremonies will announce to the group "We are now on Monday". The user will remove from the bin the number of items consumed on Monday (2), and place the items aside. This step will not be timed. The timer will then start the stop watch, and the supplies handler will complete the following steps:

1. Walk to the bin from Central Stores. Remember to record the distance.

2. Count the number of items in the bin. We're doing a strict Par Level method, where actual counting is required. Eye-balling is not permitted.

3. Calculate the difference between the Par Level and the counted quantity. On Day 1, for example, you should be short 2 pieces.

4. Walk back to the Central Stores. Again record this distance.

5. Count out the required number of items. For example, 2 will be needed on Monday.

6. Walk back to the Point of Use and place the items into the bin.

7. Walk back to Central Stores, which is "home base" for the supply handlers.

8. This completes one day of the simulation. You should have taken two round trips to and from Central Stores, completed two counting exercises (one at the Point of Use and one in Central Stores) and one replenishment cycle,

along with the respective times. Repeat this exercise for all five days and add up the numbers. We're now ready for the Kanban simulation.

Running the Kanban Simulation

In the Kanban portion of this exercise you will use exactly the same consumption pattern shown above. In preparation, however, you will count out 5 poker chips and place them in the plastic bag. You will also place 5 poker chips in Central Stores in a plastic bag. The items in the bag represent a "two-bin" Kanban system, where the first quantity is loose in the bin, and the second quantity is in a plastic bag. Explain to the group that no replenishment will be done until the last loose piece is consumed and the plastic bag is opened. Otherwise no action is required. When the plastic bag is opened and the items are placed in the bin, no counting is needed. The replenishment quantity will always be 5.

The user will notify Central Stores when a plastic bag has been opened. In this simulation you will signal verbally, but in an actual hospital the signal could be a bar-code, a Kanban reorder card, an RFID tag, a phone call or a variety of other methods. Let's go through this simulation step by step, as before.

1. The user will remove items from the bin, based on the schedule shown above. No action is required until all of the loose poker chips have

been consumed and the plastic bag needs to be opened (this will happen on Day 3). The poker chips in the bag will be placed in the bin, and the user will notify the supplies handler verbally: "We need supplies!".

2. The supplies handler does nothing until notified by the user. At that point (Wednesday in the simulation) he/she will simply pick up the plastic bag in Central Stores (previously prepared), deliver it to the Point of Use, and place it in the bin. Don't open the bag, just place it in the bin.

3. During the Kanban cycle, only 1 roundtrip to the Point of Use should be needed, and no counting at all should be done. This concludes the Kanban portion of the simulation. The data recorder should now complete the results sheet by calculating the difference between Par Level and Kanban, and the percent difference, which will be dramatic.

Post-Simulation Discussion

Here are some of the questions you should ask the group in order to stimulate discussion:

1. What would the signal to the Supplies Handler actually be in a hospital? *The choices include a telephone call, having supplies handlers come to*

pick up the Kanban cards, bar-coding, and even RFID tags as an advanced option.

2. Could the supplies handler simply pick up Kanban cards (instead of a signal to Central Stores)? Would this be more efficient that counting or eye-balling parts? *Having a Supplies Handler do a "round" to pick up or record reorder cards is a simple option, and can be done in a fraction of the time needed to count or eye-ball the bins.*

3. Does the Kanban method require more storage space? *As you saw, the storage space should be the same or less than the Par Level method. Two physical bins are not required.*

4. Could we run out of supplies 100% in either scenario? What might we do to reduce that risk? *Of course you could run out of supplies in either scenario, if usage is highly variable. That's why we like the "supermarket" concept, where an additional supply is not far away. Also evaluate the quantities stored, and increase them if necessary.*

5. Are there any reasons why a Kanban method would not work in our hospital? Why isn't this method more common in hospitals? *We wonder that ourselves. There is no good reason why Kanban should not work extremely well in hospitals.*

The results of this simulation are *dramatic*, and one of the best ways to engage hospital staff in this new way of thinking.

Chapter 2:
Batch vs. Flow in the Lab

The instructions for this simulation are written with Lab processes in mind, but they can be applied to any Value Stream in the hospital where the response time is hindered by batch processing. Batch process refers to the practice of processing or working on more than one unit at a time before the group, i.e. the batch, can move to the next step. Batch processing is highly detrimental to response time, since typically all of the items in the batch are waiting (not being worked on) most of the time.

Run 1: Batch Processing

Resources:

1. 10 Product A cards. Name these with a specific Lab test name your team is familiar with. Print out the Product A cards from the template provided in Appendix B.
2. 1 stopwatch
3. 5 colored pencils
4. Results Sheet (provided as a separate PDF)
5. 5 staff members, 1 inspector, 1 specimen handler, 1 timer

Instructions:

Place the 5 staff members and the inspector around

the room, with some distance between them, and don't line them up in assembly line fashion. Each staff member will be assigned a Lab process (use the Lab processes for the Lab test you selected for the A cards) and be given a colored pencil. The work for each staff member is to fill out the symbol corresponding with his/her workstation with the pencil. For the batch exercise all 10 cards will be completed at each workstation before they are moved to the next staff member. A specimen handler will be summoned verbally when the stack of 10 cards are ready to be moved. The timer will track two times: the time for the *first card* to be reviewed by final inspection, and the time for the *last card* to be reviewed by final inspection. The final inspector will be looking for three types of defects: an incomplete card, shapes not completely filled out, and drawing outside of the line.

Results:

Document on the results sheet the time needed to complete the first card, the time required to complete the last (10th) card, the number of rejects and the total number of people required.

Run 2: Flow Processing

Resources:

1. 10 Product A cards. Name these a with a specific Lab test name your team is familiar

with. Print these cards from the file provided in Appendix B.

2. 1 stopwatch
3. 5 colored pencils
4. Results Sheet
5. 5 staff members, 1 inspector, 1 timer

Instructions:

Place the 5 staff members and the inspector next to each other in a line. Announce to the group that the specimen handler will no longer be needed and is being reassigned to other value-added work. As before, each staff member will be assigned a Lab process (use the Lab processes for the Lab test you selected for the A cards) and be given a colored pencil. As before, the work for each staff member is to fill out the symbol corresponding with his/her workstation with the colored pencil. In this run staff members *are* allowed to move the cards to the next process one at a time, without waiting for the batch to be completed. They do not have to wait for the next staff member to be free; they can simply push their completed card to the next position. The timer and the inspector will work as before.

Results:

Document on the results sheet the time needed to complete the first card, the time required to complete the last (10th) card, the number of rejects and the total number of people required.

Discussion: Batch vs. Flow Processing

Option: Print this page to have with you as you lead the discussion.

Discussion Points:

1. The time for both the first card and the entire batch was significantly less. Why? *Because by processing specimens (or anything) in a flow vs. batch, you convert the wait time you saw at the beginning of the simulation into value-added work.*

2. Was the work well balanced? Ask the staff members to comment. *Probably not, because the shapes you have to fill out were more or less complex. Also, people have different skills and work at different speeds.*

3. Do we do any batching in our hospital? *There are a lot of batch processes in hospitals. Some are unavoidable (autoclave to sterilize instrument sets) and others should be analyzed to turn into flow processes (re-assembly of instrument sets)*

4. Does batching occur in the office, for example in departments like scheduling or accounting? *Yes, point the group towards*

paperwork processing and documents stacking up in the inboxes awaiting signature.

5. What would it take to reduce or eliminate batching in our facility? What are the reasons that we do this? *Discuss the potential need to physically redesign some departments (possible?) or to redesign the department's workflow.*

6. Were there any rejects? What was the reason for them?

7. The average number of units not actually being worked on during the batch run was around 9 pieces. Was this also true for the flow run? *No. It was very likely none or very little depending on the process balance.*

8. Was there a productivity gain between the first and second run? *Yes and No. The team could have processed many more specimens in flow mode as compared to batch mode, due primarily to the fact the they were waiting most of the time in the batch mode.*

9. We eliminated the need for a specimen handler. What should happen to this worker? *Discuss that the hospital should make a concerted effort to NOT lay off staff as a result of continuous improvement, as*

this will threaten sustainability of results and enthusiasm for continuous improvement.

10. Could the staff members themselves perform the final inspection step? *Yes. The Final Inspection process DOES NOT add value to the product. Quality should not be inspected in but rather built in. Each staff member should perform an inspection step on each specimen before letting it move to the next step. Discuss Check-Do-Check.*

Instructor Notes

Print this page to have with you as you lead the discussion.

- Set the stage: *"Welcome to the Lab at St. Elsewhere Hospital. We have been challenged to improve our response times as well as our quality. We could try several traditional approaches, like adding more staff and buying new equipment. However, we are not made of money and there are other priorities for any additional funds "*

- Do not stop the simulation for discussions. There will be time for that during the discussion portion.

- Feel free to joke around with those staff members that speed up or slow down because they are being observed.

- The audience will be tempted to talk and joke around with the staff members. Manage that aspect so it does not get out of hand. Ask the audience to pay attention to the issues you will be pointing out.

Batch run

- As soon as the Batch simulation begins, point out that the staff members in the backend processes are waiting for the first process to complete the batch. This is waste.

- Point out the different work styles. Some staff members are faster than others; others color the outside and then fill the shapes, while others are very neat.

- Indicate to the audience, that the distance between the processes in batch mode prevents staff members from quickly reacting to help each other out as they might not be able to see each other.

Flow Run

- Point out that is much easier to see each other now.

- As soon as the Flow simulation starts, point out that the wait time in the backend processes has been virtually eliminated. That will result in increased productivity.

- Indicate that performing check-do-check would be a lot easier now, since staff members are next to each other and they are not overwhelmed by a large batch.

- Make sure you point out at the accumulation of cards in between workstations and comment that this is happening due to the natural statistical imbalances (people are not robots) How can we help? Introduce the In-Process Kanban (IPK) technique (see Simulation 3).

- An IPK is a unit (or more) of inventory in-between processes that serves as a demand signal (GO) and as a way to control inventory in the value stream.

- Try the Flow run one more time by adding an IPK in between each workstation. Use one sheet of letter size paper and write a big "X" in the center. The idea is "If you can see the X , GO" or work. This will prevent the building-up of units between stations.

Chapter 3: Staff Flexing in the Sterile Processing Department

Flexing means *moving to where the work needs to be done*, and the term is derived from the expression "flexible employee". The instructions for this simulation are written with the Sterile Processing department in mind, but they can be applied to any Value Stream in the hospital where the response time is hindered by batch processing and where Staff Flexing would aid productivity. It is identical to the Batch versus Flow simulation, but with the addition of In Process Kanbans and flexible staffing.

This simulation starts with the Batch vs. Flow exercise and adds the flexing exercise at the end.

Recommended processes for this simulation are for a hand-washed set:

1. The initial stack of cards is the "Case Cart Queue" as it comes out of the "Dirty Elevator".

2. Workstation 1: Cart Breakdown

3. Workstation 2: Instrument set sorting and hand washing

4. Workstation 3: Hand-dry set

5. Workstation 4: Reassemble set

6. Workstation 5: Wrap for autoclave

Run 1: Batch Processing

Resources:

1. 10 Product A cards
2. 5 IPK cards (cards with an "X")
3. 1 stopwatch
4. 5 colored pencils
5. Results Sheet (Print from PDF)
6. 5 staff members, 1 inspector, 1 instrument set handler, 1 timer

Instructions:

Place the 5 staff members and the inspector around the room, with some distance between them. Each staff member will be assigned an SPD process and be given a colored pencil. The work for each staff member is to fill out the symbol corresponding with his/her workstation with the colored pencil. For the batch exercise all 10 cards will be completed at each workstation before they are moved to the next staff member. An Instrument Set Handler will be summoned verbally when the stack of 10 cards is ready to be moved. The timer will track two times: the time for the *first card* to be reviewed by final inspection, and the time for the *last card* to be reviewed by final inspection. The final inspector will be looking for three types of defects: an incomplete card, shapes not completely filled out, and drawing outside of the line.

Results:

Document on the results sheet the time needed to complete the first card, the time required to complete the last (10th) card, the number of rejects and the total number of people required.

Run 2: Flow Processing

Resources:

1. 10 Product A cards, as before.
2. 1 stopwatch
3. 5 colored pencils
4. Results Sheet
5. 5 staff members, 1 inspector, 1 timer

Instructions:

Place the 5 staff members and the inspector next to each other in a line. Announce to the group that the Instrument Set Handler will no longer be needed and is being reassigned to other value-added work. As before, each staff member will be assigned an SPD process and be given a colored pencil. As before, the work for each staff member is to fill out the symbol corresponding with his/her workstation with the colored pencil. In this run staff members are allowed to move the cards to the next process one at a time, without waiting for the batch to be completed. They do not have to wait for the next staff member to be free; they can simply push their completed card to the next position. The timer and the inspector will work as before.

Results:

Document on the results sheet the time needed to complete the first card, the time required to complete the last (10th) card, the number of rejects and the total number of people required.

Discussion: Batch vs. Flow Processing

Discussion Points: see the points made in Chapter 2. The discussion up to this point will be the same.

Run 3: Flow Processing with Flexing

In this simulation we will be introducing the concept of the In Process Kanban or IPK. An IPK is simply an open spot or space that is used as a signal for when to work and when to work somewhere else. The IPK acts as a traffic signal for the workflow, and causes staff members to stop and go as appropriate. You would normally have an IPK on the upstream side of your workstation, and also an IPK on the downstream side. The IPK rules of use are as follows:

1. If the IPK spot, which could be on a table or on the floor for larger items, is empty you are allowed to fill it with the next completed item.

2. If your workstation is empty, you are also allowed to continue working without flexing, even if your downstream IPK is full.

3. If your workstation *and* the IPK spot are both full, move downstream (towards the completed product) to work or help out there.

4. If you have nothing to work on at your station (your upstream IPK is empty), move upstream to work or assist there.

Use all the same resources and set up as with the Flow processing simulation. Place an IPK card on either side of each workstation. The last workstation does not need an IPK on the downstream side, since the work is now complete. Set the stage by indicating that *"Today, the Sterile Processing Department at St. Elsewhere had a sick call, so our team is not going to be complete"* Ask one of the members of the simulation team to step aside and become a member of the audience.

You now have 5 workstations and 4 staff members. Start by asking: *"How can we run this department today?"* The main option you want to make sure you debunk is the idea of redistributing the work from 5 to 4 workstations. This would make the work unpredictable and quality is sure to suffer. Explain that in a Lean process *"The work belong to the workstation, not to the individual. All the necessary resources are at the workstation"*.

Re-emphasize the usefulness of the IPKs, as they will be important for this run.

Lead the discussion to review the flexing rules:

Rule 1: ***If you have work to do at your workstation, stay at your workstation***. You know you have work to do if there is an instrument set in the upstream (prior to you) IPK and your workstation is empty.

Rule 2: ***If you have something (instrument set) to work on (waiting in the upstream IPK) but your workstation is full, flex downstream***. Point out that your workstation being full must be due to fact that the downstream workstation is not pulling work and your downstream IPK is full. *You must always move in the direction of the blockage. Only two completed units are allowed at your workstation, one in front of you and one in the IPK.*

Rule 3: ***If you have nothing to work on, flex upstream***. Point out that having nothing to work on must be due to fact that your upstream IPK is empty. That indicates the blockage is upstream from you. *You must always move in the direction of the blockage.*

Rule 4: ***The maximum number of units (instrument sets) you are allowed to have is one at the Workstation plus one at the downstream IPK***. This controls the amount of Work In Process in the system as well as the number of instrument sets at risk of quality (what if you have a batch of defective wrappers?)

Begin the run with all four team members at the front

-end workstations (1-4) and initiate flexing when the staff member at workstation four fills the workstation and IPK (Rule 2). The instructor must guide the flexing, as it will not happen naturally until staff learns the rules.

Results:

Document on the results sheet the time needed to complete the first card, the time required to complete the last (10th) card, the number of rejects and the total number of people required.

Repeat discussion points. It is not unusual for four people to achieve almost the same number of units as the original five person team!

Chapter 4: Error Proofing in the Pharmacy

The goal of this exercise is to practice critical thinking of one's own processes with an eye for potential points of failure in the processes. The processes used in this simulation toolkit are for a Pharmacy, but the apply to any set of sequential processes to deliver value to a customer (a Value Stream).

Set the stage: *"Welcome to the Pharmacy Department at St. Elsewhere. We hear complaints from the Nursing units that medications take a long time to reach the units. We also hear that the Nurses have a hard time finding the medications we know were delivered. It seems that we have to take a critical look at how we process MD Med orders and how we pick and deliver those medications to the Nursing Units, so they can reach the patients in the fastest yet safest manner".*

Drive the discussion towards the tool(s) that would serve better in accomplishing these goals. Due to the number of unknowns and the multiple processes involved in the delivery and administration of medications to patients, the technique of choice for this analysis is *Value Stream Mapping*.

Once you reach agreement with the audience, continue: *"Since the issues at hand come from RNs in the Nursing Units and not from patients, we will* consider the RN as the Customer and the Value Stream will end with the delivery of the medication".

Continue: "At St. Elsewhere, a large number of the complaints come from the delivery of medications via the pneumatic tube system. You all have copies of the Value Stream Map (VSM) created by the team that was in charge of the mapping portion. They asked us to focus solely on opportunities for the application of techniques to improve the quality of this value stream".

Distribute copies of the two Value Stream Maps that you will find as a separate PDF available in Appendix B.

Review the VSM with the team step by step. Notice that you have two copies of the same VSM. One is the hand-drawn VSM and the second one is the cleaned-up version entered into a flow-charting software tool. The second version includes all of the *Kaizen Bursts* identified by the VSM team, so do not worry about those in this exercise. Note that specialized software is not needed, but it can be a useful and time-saving tool.

Reducing Errors: Two Methods

In this simulation you will be applying two methods for error-reduction and elimination: **poka-yoke** (Japanese for error proofing) and **check-do-check** (error catching). It is always better to prevent an error than to catch it after the fact, but what is *not* acceptable is for an error to go undetected. The purpose of this simulation is to practice the application of these methods to an actual Value Stream Map.

The Check-Do-Check process simply means that before starting work (with a patient, with a physician order, etc.) you want to make sure that the information and work coming to you is 100% correct. This is the first check. You then do your work, per a *Standard Work Definition or Standard Operating Procedure*. You then check your *own* work, in the manner prescribed by the Standard Work Definition. In this way every critical work step has been looked at by *two sets of eyes*. This does require a bit of extra time, but the time investment is well worth it and in fact necessary if there is the possibility of error.

Poka-yoke is a big topic, with a large number of books written on the subject. For your purposes in this simulation, team members should think about ways in which the potential error can be *permanently* eliminated. There are a variety of ways to accomplish this, but the principal point is that the poka-yoke improvement makes it virtually impossible to make an error on that step. Poka-yoke is clearly what you would like to achieve if possible, through a redesign of the process. Slogans or admonitions to try harder do not qualify as poka-yoke.

The Simulation

As a first pass, review the Value Stream Map as provided with the team. Be familiar with this VSM ahead of time. Read each process and describe where the process is consumed. Ignore the *Kaizen Bursts* on the electronic VSM, as these refer to process improvement projects identified by the team. Then for each process, go through the following steps:

1. Can an error occur at this process? If yes, list on the white board or flip chart the potential errors that might occur.

2. For each of the potential errors (or process failures) that could occur, identify if the error is a candidate for error-proofing, for check-do-check, or both.

3. Continue through all of the processes, and develop the list of potential errors on the white board.

4. Drill down on a few of the potential errors that were identified as candidates for error-proofing. Discuss with the team how this might be done.

5. Drill down on a few of the potential errors that were identified as candidates for check -do-check. Discuss how this could be accomplished.

Once the analysis portion of the simulation has been

done, shift the discussion to actual Value Streams within the hospital that the team can identify as in need of this type of analysis. Emphasize that simply identifying needs does nothing per se to resolve the issues, and that the Kaizen approach to process improvement has been found to be the most effective in achieving improvements in a short period of time.

Chapter 5: Sequencing for Outpatient Procedures

The purpose of this simulation is to demonstrate the benefits of intelligent sequencing or scheduling of patient procedures, in order to balance the work flow and work time. There will be five "departments" or steps in the OR Value Stream, including:

Registration, Pre-surgery, Surgery, PACU, Recovery, Discharge

Each one of the cards represents a patient moving through the various processes in the Outpatient Value Stream. The procedure time for each department is determined by the number of symbols that need to be filled in, and it varies by card.

Resources Needed:

1. 5 Product A cards, 2 Product B cards, 3 Product E cards. Print quantity needed from file provided.
2. 1 stopwatch
3. 5 colored pencils
4. Results Sheet
5. 6 department staff members, 1 timer

Run 1: Batch by Patient Type

Place the 5 departments next to each other in a line. Each department will be assigned a department name (see above) and be given a colored pencil. The work for each department is to fill out the symbol or symbols corresponding with his/her outpatient value stream task with the colored pencil. In this first run departments are not allowed to move the cards to the next department until the next person is free to work on it. The timer will track two times: the time for the first card ("patient") to be reviewed and discharged by the discharge department, and the time for the last card to be reviewed by the discharge department. The discharge department will be looking for three types of defects: an incomplete card shapes not completely filled out, and drawing outside of the line.

The sequence for the production of Patient cards is as follows:

E, E, E, B, B, A, A, A, A, A

Results:

Document on the results sheet the time needed to complete the first card, the time required to complete the last (10th) card, the number of rejects and the total number of people required.

Run 2: Sequenced

As before, place the 5 departments next to each other in a line. As before, each department will be assigned a department name and be given a colored pencil. As before, the work for each staff member is to fill out the symbol or symbols corresponding with his/her department with the colored pencil. As before, a department is not allowed to more the card to the next department until the person at the next station is free to work on it. The first department must follow the sequence of the patient cards as they are provided. The timer will work as before.

The sequence for the production of Patient cards is as follows:

A, A, E, B, A, A, E, E, B, A

Results:

Document on the results sheet the time needed to complete the first card, the time required to complete the last (10th) card, the number of rejects and the total number of people required.

Discussion Points :

1. Which of the runs achieved better patient throughput time? Why? *Instructor note: you expect better patient flow when you alternate the harder and easier procedures. Is this something that can be done by your scheduling department?*

2. Was the work well balanced? Ask the departments to comment. Can we expect work to ever be balanced between departments? How could we balance the work flow if the work times are significantly

different for each process? Instructor note: think in terms of the number of resources needed. For example, if you can prep one patient an hour, but the average surgery time is two hours, you would need at least two surgical suites to "balance" the flow.

3. What would be the result of allowing departments to simply move the patient to the next department, without waiting for an opening?

Chapter 6: Quick Changeover in the Cath Lab

The Quick Changeover in the Cath Lab simulation is an introduction to the process of reducing changeover time in a hospital process. The data used is based on an actual Quick Changeover project, and the example is the changeover process for an adult patient setup. The steps documented here are for illustration purposes only, and are not provided as examples of a "correct" procedure.

Document needed: Standard Work Definition for Cath Lab OR Setup (Excel file link provided in Appendix B).

Introduction to the Simulation

Part of the Quick Changeover process includes knowing how to document a changeover process, using the Standard Work Definition form. We have provided this document as an Excel file, and the format can be used on your Quick Changeover projects. Explain briefly the purpose of each of the columns in the spreadsheet:

1. **Order.** The sequence in which the changeover steps are done.

2. **Description of the Work Performed**. A brief description of the work step. More documentation may be needed, but on this

form keep it short.

3. **Divisible?** This is a Yes/No column that asks if the work can be done by more than one person, or if the work can be handed off to another person in mid-stream. This is good to know if you want to balance the work flow by having other resources help when needed.

4. **Machine Time.** If equipment is used, record the time in this column.

5. **Person Time**. Record the labor time required to complete the work step. A typical unit of measure is minutes, and for most purposes this is accurate enough. The time should be a "reasonable and generous" time, and not the time for the fastest or slowest person.

6. **Transport**. Record here the transport distance that may be associated with that work step.

7. **TQM Check and Self-Check**. If the work step can be done more than one way, but only one way is the right way, then a self-check will be needed. This typically takes for form of "Verify that ...." If the work step is critical, i.e. an error will have serious or

life-threatening consequences, a "TQC Check" will be needed. This is a "second set of eyes", another person, verifying that the work step was done correctly.

Step 1: Separate Internal from External

Go over the list of work steps with an eye to the following: are there any steps that can be done ahead of time, while the previous patient is still in the room? Examples of this include locating and staging any supplies and equipment needed for the next procedure ahead of time, and ensuring that any paperwork is complete. The pre-procedure needs to be complete, of course, before the patient can be brought to the room.

In the example provided, all of the steps are "internal" steps, i.e. as the process is currently designed, the steps cannot be done ahead of time. Keep in mind, however, that it is not unusual to find that 30-50% of the changeover time in hospitals is related to items that could be done ahead of time, but are not.

Step 2: Convert Internal to External

In this step of the Quick Changeover process an attempt is made to move steps that are currently internal to become external. Typically something will need to be changed in the current process that will allow this to happen. Review each of the steps in the procedure, and discuss as a team the opportunities to convert internal to external steps. The team should be encouraged to think boldly. It does not matter if the idea seems impractical or too expensive; just get the ideas on a list. Here are some suggestions for the Patient Setup list of work steps:

1. Can the patient be moved to the operating table outside of the cath room, with a table on wheels? That would reduce 4 minutes of preparation time.

2. Are there any other steps that could be done prior to the patient entering the room?

Remember that we are not discussing how things are done today, but rather brainstorming opportunities that will require changes and approvals.

Step 3: Streamline

Go over the list of work steps a third time, with an eye to "streamlining" or improving the work flow. Streamlining may involve new technology, or simply finding a more efficient way to complete the work steps, and will require the involvement of people who know the process steps well. Remember that reducing time does not mean increased stress or rushing, which increases errors. Processes will be streamlined by eliminating waste and developing creative new ways to do things.

One of the most fruitful opportunities for streamlining is related to proper sequencing of steps, so that the team is always focused on the "critical path". If the steps on the critical path are completed one by one, the total elapsed time will always be shortest possible time. If the various team members (RN, SCRUB, and PHYSICIAN) are *not* focused on the critical path, the elapsed time will be longer. Another way of looking at the critical path is to try to do as much work as possible in parallel. As a team exercise on a white board, lay out in Gantt chart format the work steps for each person, and determine if there are any opportunities to do more work in parallel.

Chapter 7: Patient Room Changeover

The purpose of this patient room changeover simulation is to train the team in the technique of "spaghetti diagramming", and how this method can be used to improve the work flow of a room changeover. The data used for this exercise is from an actual room changeover Kaizen event held at a hospital, so all of the data is real, although the sequence of steps has been changed. Note that some time is needed for cleaning chemicals to soak, which is normally around 15 minutes. Shown below is the spaghetti diagram created during that activity.

Hand-outs: A blank layout of the patient room, and a list of the work steps (current state). These forms should be printed prior to the exercise.

Task 1: Create the spaghetti diagram. All participants in the workshop can develop their own spaghetti diagram. Have one participant read off the work steps, with the first step starting in the doorway of the room. Connect the various areas of the room where work is being performed, without picking up the pen or pencil. Remind participants that this would normally be done observing actual workers, and not working from a list of work steps. When done, display several examples of the diagrams and share with the class.

Task 2: Lead a discussion session on opportunities for improving the work flow in patient room changeovers. Topics for discussion include the following:

1. Are all of the steps in the optimal order? Could some of them be rearranged to reduce walking distance?

2. Could two people, working as a team, complete the work in less than half the time of one person? (This would need to be tried out.)

3. Is the room itself arranged optimally, or are there changes to the room layout that would reduce the "spaghetti" quality of the diagrams?

4. Does the spaghetti diagram create a "call to action", when it becomes clear how much walking is needed?

5. Are there any opportunities to do any of the steps ahead of time (separate internal from external steps)?

6. Are there any opportunities to convert any of the internal steps (steps that must be done without a patient in the room) to external steps (steps that can be done ahead of time)?

7. Are there any opportunities to streamline (make more efficient) the steps shown on the list?

Example of an OR Suite Changeover Spaghetti Diagram

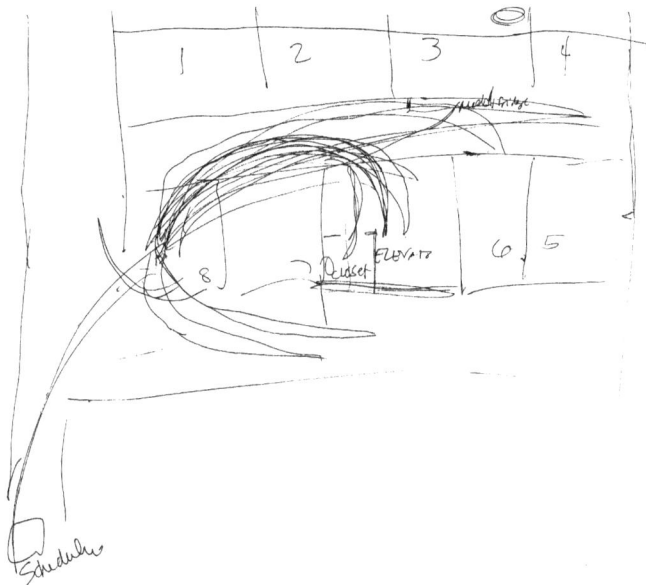

Chapter 8: The Red Bead Game

The Red Bead Game was developed by Dr. W. Edwards Deming to illustrate the fact that quality is a function of the process or value stream's capability. Slogans, Rewards/Punishments, and other external stimuli, driven by Management theories, are not likely to have any impact on quality.

This is a clever demonstration of the futility of most management systems for improving quality. Dr. Deming used to refer to it as *a stupid experiment that you'll never forget*. The experiment is described in a form similar to Dr. Deming's presentation in his seminars. As will be described at the end, it can also be adopted for very small groups and even a one on one presentation. Here's what you'll need:

1. Table with room for 4 people
2. 2 flipcharts and markers
3. 2 candy bars to use as "awards"
4. A bowl with an assortment of both red and white beads. See Appendix B for a source for these beads.
5. A 4 oz. specimen cup
6. A flat dish (for counting the beads)

Instructions:

Set up a small table in the middle of the front of the room with the red bead game set. Place conspicuously on the same table, on the side facing the audience, two candy bars.

Prepare ahead of time a flip chart sheet with some

banal slogan written on it in very large print. Try something like "Quality is Numero Uno!" or "Let's hear it for QUALITY!". Place this sheet so that it is concealed but can be displayed quickly. Learn the following script so that you can deliver it naturally and in your own style.

*Now I am going to invite you to join with me in Dr. Deming's Red Bead Game. When Dr. Deming used to teach his four-day seminar, he introduced the Red Bead exercise on the third day, when everyone **else** was exhausted. He invited the participants to relax and take a little recess, a little time for relaxation and enjoyment. So here we go (assume the role of the Pharmacy Director)...*

*I am the Director of the **White Bead Pharmacy** at [**your name**] Hospital/Medical Center. We deliver medication to our patients in the form of pure white beads, untouched by human hands. I have been given a process to Order, Pick, Check, and Deliver white beads designed by... I am not sure, but it is the way we have always done it! It is perfect, and will not be changed.*

To deliver these meds/beads, I need some staff members, and I'm going to ask for volunteers from the group here to help me in this critical patient care endeavor.

*First I need people for whom there are **no** job requirements (no education requirements, no experience requirements) you just have to be willing workers. So can I get four people to volunteer to be willing workers?*

If you don't get any volunteers, go ahead and pick them one at a time saying: *"**Why, thank you, George. Come on up.**"* Until you get your four people.

Now I have two jobs with requirements: you have to know how to write numbers up to 20. Does anybody in this organization meet that requirement? These jobs are for people who like to record other people's mistakes. What I need are **two inspectors**. *Please bring with you paper and a pencil.*

Now I need someone who likes to tell other people what to do, the **Senior Inspector**

And finally, I need two people who can both write and add, may be even up to 100. These are my two **recorders**.

Assemble the nine volunteers so that the four workers are to the right of the table with beads (as you face the audience), the two inspectors and the Senior Inspector are to the left, and the two recorders are standing at the flipcharts with the Chart and Table, which were prepared ahead of time, at the back.

Pharmacy staffers, will you line up over here, please [at the table, to the right]? And recorder number one, will you please write down their names on the table in rows 1 through 4?

Ready for training?

We pick, check, and deliver our meds/white beads by dipping this cup [demonstrate] into the beads in the bowl, letting the beads roll into the cup, and then withdrawing the cup at exactly 47 degrees. If you do it right, you end up with all white beads in the cup. [Withdrawing the cup]. Now I have allowed some defects so that you'll know what they look like.

Pour the bead into a flat dish carefully, and show the dish to the four willing workers. Then show it to the two inspectors. They count the number of red beads, and record their findings separately on a sheet of paper. The Senior Inspector compares the numbers shown to him by the two inspectors and calls out in a loud voice the number of defects. He/she then dismisses the worker who returns to the beginning of the line. Meanwhile, the first recorder writes the number of defects in the first box, totaling the numbers as columns and rows are completed, and the second inspector plots the number on his chart. [Show the recorders where the numbers and dots should be put.]

*Now as you can see, we will do three days of work. Each worker will have one turn per day. At this Pharmacy, our main goal is **quality**; but we also believe in **high productivity**, so there will be no talking! We discovered long ago that allowing staffers to chit-chat distracts them from hard work. Now we wouldn't want that, would we?*

Allow the workers to go through one turn. Badger them constantly. After the first one is finished, draw him aside as if for a confidential chat and tell him, speaking loud enough to be heard by all, that the objective is *no* defects, not the number he got. Keep reminding them to withdraw the cup at exactly 47 degrees. Generally be obnoxious, bossy, and condescending. For example:

Wait, wait, stop. This isn't going at all well. I know what's wrong. We need a slogan, a battle cry. [Display the flip chart sheet with the slogan on it] Now: all say it after me...Quality is Numero Uno! [or whatever you have used] Now, are you feeling inspired? Good! Let's begin day two!

Continue haranguing the workers. Ask one after he has finished if he has a family. Ask another why she isn't any good at beads... anything you can think of to pressure the staffers. It sometimes helps to pick one out for punishment and keep picking on him or her. Just be obnoxious.

This is still isn't working. Hold it. I know. We don't have an awards program. Let's establish one right now. Let's see who has the lowest defects in a single turn? George! Please come forward. On behalf of the White Bead Pharmacy and {your name] Hospital/Medical Center, I want to publicly reward you for your exemplary work. [Give him a candy bar]. Can we have a round of applause for George? Now let's see who has shown the greatest improvement....Sally! Come on right up here...isn't she great?...Well, for your great improvement in your work, I want to publicly reward you on behalf of the White Bead Pharmacy and [your name] Hospital/Medical Center. Can we hear it for this fine lady? [Lead the applause].

OK, back to work. The last day! Let's see how much we can all improve

Continue the badgering, with remarks about how some people don't appreciate rewards.

Well, folks, since we are not delivering perfect meds in the form of pure white beads, [your name] Hospital/ Medical Center has decided to outsource the Pharmacy, so I have to let you all go. [Fire each group individually].

While one person does the calculations (shown below), complete the exercise by asking each participant how he felt about what was going on. Ask how much control she had, how he might have improved the process if he had been allowed. Ask if any of them have ever experienced anything like this (for example, recording data that are never used). The point is that management had complete control of the process, the staffers had none. And yet management rewarded and punished them as if they were in control. Ask what effect the slogan and the rewards had. Ask about the performance of the Pharmacy Director. Ask if they have ever seen any managers like him.

Mark the values on chart.

Now what we have constructed here is a run chart. You can see that when I join the dots [do it]. But we can turn it into a control chart by showing the average and the upper and lower control limits.

Mark Upper and Lower Control Limits on Chart.

What this shows is that the red bead process is in control [if it's out of control, see below]. If a process is in control, it's ready to be improved. If it's out of statistical control, then it's either in the midst of change or it's being impinged upon by something outside of the process itself. So what we need to do is work on the larger environment that the process is embedded in first, then, after the process is in control, work on improving it. In other words, don't bother trying to improve a process that's not in statistical control.

Average	$\bar{x} = \dfrac{TotalDefects}{12(numberoftrials)}$
Proportion	$\bar{p} = \dfrac{TotalDefect}{600(numberofbeadsdrawn)}$
UCL	$UCL = \bar{x} + 3\sqrt{x(\bar{p} - 1)}$
Lower Control Limit	$LCL = \bar{x} - 3\sqrt{x - (\bar{p} - 1)}$

Now see these high and low peaks in the control chart? They're within the control limits. Notice how I (or my partner) kept haranguing the workers over these scores. I rewarded George for this low score, and I scolded Helen for this high score. And yet what I was rewarding and scolding was nothing more than random variation over which the workers had no control whatsoever!

Let's find out what caused these outliers. George, what happened here?

[Find out what was going on. I have always been able to explain all the outliers either by the fact that the process was changing (e.g., the workers lost heart and stopped trying) or there was an outside influence (sometimes I get the players so upset that they start shaking--then *I'm* the outside influence messing up the system). Then proceed with the remainder of the explanation shown above.

It is the process, not the people in the process. If you wan to improve performance improve the process.	Do not attempt to fix the process by automating. In some RARE cases this may work, but they are the exception. Fix the process, then automate.
Quality starts at the top. Top Management must own the value streams and processes.	Stay away from "We all own the value streams and processes" that is a sure path to short-lived results.
Numerical goals and standards are meaningless, unless supported by capable processes and value streams.	Stay away from unrealistic goals. Do not "shoot for the moon" if you can barely walk.
External motivation has limited reach.	Rewards and punishments are not a sustainable way of ensuring results.
People are not always the main cause of variability.	A bad process produces bad outcomes regardless of how hard you try.
Slogans, exhortations, posters, and battle cries are at best useless and normally harmful.	Allow staff members to find joy in a job well done, by delivering quality care to patients. That is why they are in healthcare.
Respect the staff members.	The best way to show respect and to tell people that they ARE the Hospital's most valuable asset is by involving them in Continuous Improvement.

Chapter 9: Spreadsheet Simulations

Sometimes a manual simulation as shown in the previous chapters, is good but not sufficient. A question that will probably arise out of the Par Versus Kanban simulation, for example, is "how much money can we save?". As a manager I may be convinced that the Kanban method is superior, based on the results of the hands-on exercise, but how big is the potential benefit? Should I put the conversion on the back-burner, or move it to the front of the line, based on the size of the expected savings? For this type of analysis a spreadsheet is a great tool. Just about everyone is familiar with spreadsheets, and since the calculations are instantaneous you can do a variety of "what if" calculations with varying assumptions. You can determine how optimistic or conservative you want to be in your analysis. You may want to create a number of different scenarios for comparison, and apply probabilities to each scenario. If the potential benefit is big enough, why would you want to wait to implement it? Remember that a million-dollar savings represents about *$80,000 per month* down the drain in the form of waste.

Don't worry, in this chapter you won't need to be a spreadsheet guru to explore the possibilities for using computer spreadsheets to do some simulation exercises. We'll be providing you with a sample game that you can play with and use, which may give you some ideas for other games you can create yourself, but no profound technical expertise is required. The beauty of a spreadsheet game is that it allows the user to experiment with many different scenarios, and get instant feedback regarding the results. The calculations and formulas we will be using are basic arithmetic.

A spreadsheet simulation is what we call a "static" simulation, in that for a given set of assumptions, we'll always get the same answer. This is different from a full computer simulation model that adds variability to the results, in order to simulation real-world conditions more accurately. While creating a dynamic simulation model could certainly be valuable, this requires a high level of expertise, and is best left to the computer simulation experts.

There are three steps to complete in creating a spreadsheet simulation. First we need to define the **inputs**, the data that we will need to collect and that we will be manipulating. Some of this data will be static, i.e. it won't be changing during the simulation. Other data will be dynamic, and we will be "playing with" these numbers to create a reasonable and believable model. Second, we will be doing some **calculations** based on the data provided. In most cases we're talking about addition, subtraction,

Par vs Kanban Benefits Calculator Beta 1.0

Click Here for an Explanation

Performance Results

Viability of Counting Method: Not Viable

Viability of Eyeball Method: Viable

Yearly Waste of Nurses Time	$168,068
Yearly Value of Supplies Handler Time Savings	$584,798
Total Yearly Waste Reduction	$752,866
Waste Reduction due to Reduce Shortages	$267,430
Waste Reduction due to Reduced Handling	$405,436

LEAN HOSPITAL

	Par Level	Kanban
Counting Hours Per Day	55	
Counting FTEs Per Day	7.5	
Eyeball Hours Per Day	11.6	
Eyeball FTEs Per Day	4.5	
Picking Hours Per Day	46.0	24.9
Picking FTEs Per Day	6.3	3.0

	Par Level	Kanban
Items Out of Stock Per Day:	131.6	0.62
Time to Respond (Hours):	17.5	0.11
FTEs Required to Respond:	2.4	0.015

Data Entry

Number of Supplies Handlers	8
Number of Items	478
Hourly Labor Rate, Supplies Handler	$18.76
Nurse Labor Rate, Nurse	$42.00
Number of Stocked/Counted Items	3,289

Estimated Time to Count (Seconds)	60
Estimated Time to Eyeball (Seconds)	12
Percent of Items Reaching Replenishment	40%
Picking Time Per Item (Minutes)	2

Percent of Items Out of Stock	4%
Stockout Response Time (Minutes)	9
Nurses Time Per Stockout (Minutes)	5
Kanban Replenishment Interval (Days)	5

multiplication and division. Finally, we will be **calculating the benefits**, converting our results (as much as possible) into dollars. The beauty of using a spreadsheet is that we can manipulate the variables to our heart's content, with the goal of developing a model that we and others can believe in.

We have provided you with a live example of this type of simulation model, which you can access and run at:

www.leanhospitalgroup.com/webinars/KanbanCalulator.swf

You will need internet access and your computer must be able to run Flash programs; 99% of PCs have Flash installed, but talk to your network administrator if you have problems. Following is an explanation of this simulation tool.

Step 1: Determine Static Data

The static data used in the model include the following:

1. **Number of Supplies Handlers.** How many FTEs do you have restocking items in your hospital?

2. **Number of Nurses.** If supplies are not available, nurses time will be impacted. How many nurses do you have that could be affected by shortages?

3. **Hourly Rates for Supplies Handlers and Nurses.** Use an average hourly rate for these two labor categories.

4. **Number of Unique Supplies Locations.** This is the number of locations that need to be restocked. The same item can be stored in multiple locations.

These static items will typically not change during the different simulation scenarios that you will be creating.

Step 2: Determine Dynamic Data

These are the data elements that you will be "playing with", in order to create conservative, medium or optimistic scenarios. In this Flash-based tool you can use the slider or drop-down tools to change the values. In a normal spreadsheet you would simply enter the new value into the spreadsheet cell in order to change the value.

1. **Estimated Time to Count.** How long does it take to count, not eyeball, a single item? This is going to vary quite a bit, but come up with an average time. In this model the range of time is between 0 and 60 seconds.

2. **Estimated Time to Eyeball.** If your supplies handlers don't actually count, and they probably don't, then estimate the time required to eyeball a

single item. The range in this model is between 0 and 12 seconds.

3. **Percent of Items Needing Replenishment.** On any give day, what percentage of the total supplies locations need restocking? The range in this model is between 0 and 100%.

4. **Picking Time Per Item.** Estimate the time required to retrieve an item from Central Stores, including an allocation for the transportation time to and from the storage locations.

5. **Percent of Items Out of Stock.** On any given day, how many items (across all locations) are out of stock and require a special restocking? If you don't have this data, some data collection may be necessary.

6. **Stockout Response Time.** How long does it take to respond to a stockout, i.e. how long is the material handler occupied in responding to the shorage? This will include time to field the request, find the item, and deliver it to the right location.

7. **Nurses Time Per Stockout.** How much of a nurses time is needed to respond to a stockout? Included here is the time to walk, make a phone call, and otherwise be distracted from primary

duties. Remember that we're looking for average time, as individual times will vary.

8. **Kanban Replenishment Interval.** Set a target inventory level for common supplies, in days of usage. Remember that for inexpensive items we are more concerned about storage space and not running out, than about the cost of the supplies, which will usually be less than 10% of your total hospital material cost. Three to five days is a good target for these kinds of items.

Step 2: Performing Calculations

The next step in creating your spreadsheet-based model is to do some simple calculations, based on the data you have previously defined. In this model we're doing the following arithmetic:

1. **Counting Hours Per Day**. Multiply the time to count one item times the number of unique locations and items.

2. **Counting FTEs Per Day**. The total time per day needed to count, divided by the time in an average working day.

3. **Eyeball Hours Per Day**. Multiply the time to eyeball one item times the number of unique locations and items.

4. **Eyeball FTEs Per Day**. The total time per day

needed to eyeball, divided by the time in an average working day.

5. **Picking Hours Per Day**. The picking time per item times the number of unique locations and items times the percent of items needed replenishment.

6. **Picking FTEs Per Day**. The total time per day needed to pick parts, divided by the time in an average working day.

7. **Items Out of Stock Per Day**. The total number of unique locations and items, times the percentage of items out of stock.

8. **Time to Respond (Hours).** The number of items out of stock per day times the stockout response time.

9. **FTEs Required to Respond**. The Time to Respond divided by the time in a average working day.

Step 3: Calculate the Benefits.

In this model there are two blocks in the Performance Results section of the dashboard. The first is a visual cue regarding the viability of the selected counting and eyeball methods. If the percent of FTE times exceeds 25% of the total FTE material handling time available (this was one of the data points defined in Step 1), then classify the settings as "Not Viable", or not possible with the current level of staffing.

The second section of the Benefit Calculation compares the Kanban method with the Par Level method, and multiplies the difference in hours by the average labor rate for both Supplies Handlers and Nurses. The number of replenishment cycles for the Kanban method is substantially less than the Par Method, and we expect stock-outs to also be reduced to close to zero. An Excel spreadsheet available as a download with this book in Appendix B shows the calculations done in this section of the simulation model.

The beauty of allowing the uses to modify the assumptions is that they can develop ownership of the results, as opposed to a rosy picture presented by someone else, or (horrors) a consultant.

What other types of spreadsheet models might be appropriate? Just about every example shown in this book would be a good candidate. We've already covered Chapter 1, but there should be tangible and quantifiable benefits associated with all of the manual simulations presented here, with the possible exception of the Red Bead Game. Give it a try, and please share your questions and work with us!

Appendix A: Sample Forms

Value Stream Map Hand-Drawn

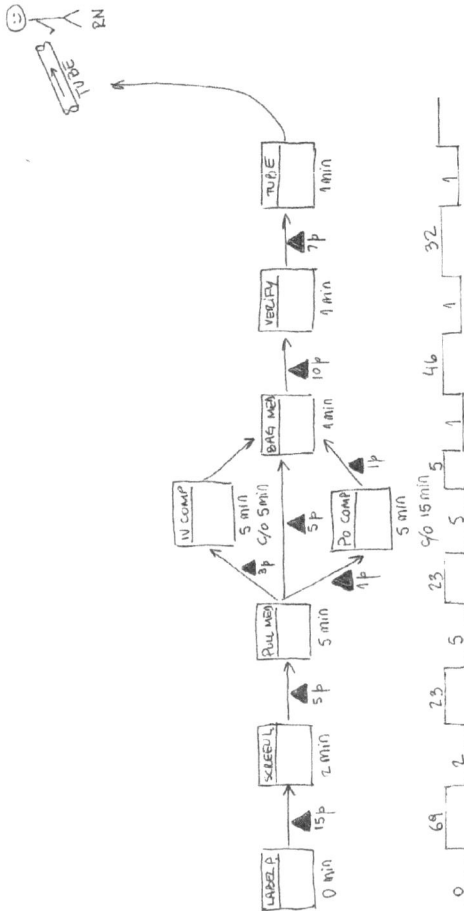

METRIC	PAR	KANBAN	DIFFERENCE	PERCENT
Number of Supplies Counted Per Day				
Time Spent Counting Supplies (Seconds)				
Number of Replenishment Cycles (Trips)				
Time Spent Replenishing Supplies (Seconds)				
Distance Traveled (Feet or Meters)				
Total Elapsed Time				

Value Stream Map Computer-Drawn Example

Quick Changeover Map

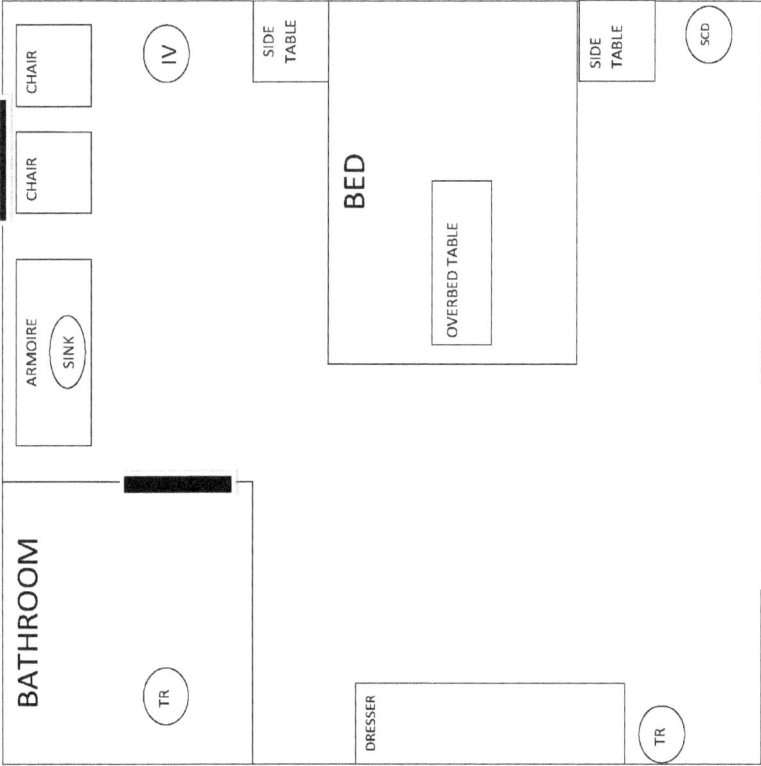

Appendix B: Download Forms

Full-size examples of the various forms and exhibits shown in this book can be downloaded from the Lean Hospital website by entering the following URL into your browser:

www.leanhospitalgroup.com/document/leantools.zip

After the download, unzip the file to a folder on your PC.

Lean Hospital Group

The Lean Hospital Group is an association of like-minded organizations with the mission of promoting Lean principles and tools in hospitals. Leonardo Group Americas is a founding member.

Leonardo Group Americas LLC (LGA)

The authors are the Principals with Leonardo Group Americas, LLC. The mission of *Leonardo Group Americas* is to assist its hospital clients to achieve success with the implementation of advanced Lean methods. This is accomplished through our talented staff and their profound knowledge and experience, a suite of world-class training seminars, state of the art web-based training, certification programs, books and materials, and through the prudent application of Lean software tools.

LGA has been involved with the deployment of Lean in hospitals since 2002, and is a founding member of the Lean Hospital Group. They have conducted Lean improvement projects in virtually every hospital process and Value Stream.

Find out more about Leonardo Group Americas at

www.leonardogroupamericas.com

and

www.leanhospitalgroup.com

or send us an email at

contact@leonardogroupamericas.com

www.ingramcontent.com/pod-product-compliance
Lightning Source LLC
Chambersburg PA
CBHW071609200326
41519CB00021BB/6934